Bury your horses
Kelsey Marie Harris

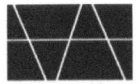

Bury Your Horses ©2020 by **Kelsey Marie Harris**. Published in the United States by Vegetarian Alcoholic Press. Not one part of this work may be reproduced without expressed written consent from the author. For more information, please contact vegalpress@gmail.com

Contents:

Bury Your Horses..................3

for James,
my father,
a hard working man

Paint it green
and bury the horse
under the porch
with the others.

The vibrator in the night stand is a microphone,

not to be confused with a megaphone.

The vibrator is not to be confused.

Love is a luxury
like avocados
and toilet paper.

Massage my millennial mouth,
naked

in the storefront.
So long as you pay
your rent on time.

So long as you keep
the lights on.

Coffee stains
on the drop ceiling
make me insecure
about my teeth.

My jaw clicks
when I stare into your eyes.

Maybe on account
of the frog gig in your retina.

As tadpoles
we threw seed pods
into each other's backs
and set the fields on fire.

When we weren't watching
Space Jam.

The soup was made
from grass clippings.

It never gave you flight,

so we smoked dead leaves
rolled in notebook paper.

There's always a box
of dead kittens in the garage.

A live one pissing
in the basement.

A boy would be a gun

if the barrel smelled
like weed and peanut butter.

If I'm on my period
and I lie to you,

I'm on my rag bologna.

You'd understand if you knew
to spell it without any R's.

If you knew you could
circle the parking lot
but you won't avoid
the clowns.

Quitting while you're ahead
is not conducive to time travel.

Paint your horse yellow.

Bury it under the swing
where we showed each other
our genitals.

The best pot for crying
is the kettle with wings.

Pour your tears
in the community pool
with the others.

Self care as an act of war
is more violent than combat
hand to hand or with guns.

The van is waiting out back.

The women have books
and AK 47s, as back up.

The crawl space
is the perfect size for children.

The dirt in my nails
is my attempt at escaping.

The virus lived three days
on the light switch,

now your sister is dead.

The government won't collect
the body.

Sheets once new
collect skin samples.

Viral as a dance.

Viral as a sperm count.

Viral as decay
and cheap vacations.

Paint the horse grey

and bury it in the schoolyard

near the steps
where the slow boy
serenades you
with B2K lyrics.

On the last day
we build trenches,

abandon the lines in the sand.

Find solace in a canoe ride
after your mother dies.
Next summer a boy drowns
in the same river.

Irony tastes like

leaving your drink
alone at a party.

Now you carry
a basketball in a paper bag,

ask for change
outside the laundry mat,

cradle a babydoll
on the city bus.

According to the algorithm,
there's always a kid
with cancer,

a girl giving head
in the stairwell,

a teacher
who can't hide their vices.

The ecstasy is mixed
with the Altoids
and the garbage cans
are on fire.

You aren't who you were
except sometimes

between the lines
in the notes you pass me

under the table.

You want to tell me
we're going the wrong way,

but hindsight says
I should be the last to know.

Paint it blue
and bury the horse
next to the old Mustang
broke down in the yard.

Only because I like the irony.

Only because I hate
the raccoon family
that lives there.

Maybe
this might drive them
out of town.

Unless
they hate horses
and therefore appreciate
the irony, too.

In which case, they can stay.

I'm trying to achieve
a new level of introversion
I can't reach living in a house.

The yard
is "off the grid" enough
to still have WIFI
and not have to feel
like a person.

I don't want
to identify as human.

They didn't put that option
on the Census form.

The grass in the yard
has grown tall enough,

no one will walk back there.

Life imitates art.
Yard imitates life.
Yard imitates vagina.

Fill in the blanks.

If you don't know
what to write,

check your homophones.

If you don't know what
this is all about, check me.

I need to be put in my place,

spanked, even.

I don't know
if we're in Kansas anymore,
or if we ever were, even.

I'm art drunk. Pretending
to read all the books.

Taking mugs of wine
and coffee to the face, now.

I'm stranded between
Tuesday and Saturday.
I'd write to you but I've "air-
fried" my hands and my pens.

Paint it red.
Then bury the horse.
Probably in that spot
you tried to plant a Skittle
tree.

20 minutes playing
hide and seek with a squirrel
and I don't know
who's stupider, for it.

All the boys I thought I loved
were mentally challenged.

I didn't know until later.
No one told me.

Probably because they
assumed I was too.

They were right.
I didn't know until later.

Later, it seems,
is always right now. I wonder
what I'm currently oblivious to.

I remember everything
I've repressed in vivid detail.

The thing I'd like
to remember, I've forgotten.

My storage space is low.

Apparently I'm not the admin.

Lately I've been questioning
the idea of who I think I am,
if I don't exist.

There are never enough
hours in our imaginary day.

No one
has had the bright Idea

of making up more.

We accept
what we've been told.

Even when the evidence
coughs in our face.

I've buried all my horses
and swallowed
all the Goddamned paint.

I don't want to die
burdened by logic.

I've got enough baggage
to carry through the gates.

Heaven has a small room for sinners with good intentions.

Kelsey Marie Harris has no degrees or accolades. She paints and writes poetry fueled from overthinking, anxiety, and general self-loathing. Her chapbook *The Jolly Queef* was published by Vegetarian Alcoholic Press. Her full length poetry book, *Spit (verb) in my mouth* is forthcoming from Vegetarian Alcoholic Press, as well. She has also had work published in The Rust Mill, TLDR magazine, Horror Sleaze Trash, and Forklift Ohio.

www.ingramcontent.com/pod-product-compliance
Lightning Source LLC
Chambersburg PA
CBHW030139100526
44592CB00011B/961